Long Ago AND Far Away

The Aztecs

Michael DeMocker

PURPLE TOAD
PUBLISHING

Printing
1   2   3   4   5   6   7   8   9

Ancient China
Ancient Egypt
Ancient Rome
The Aztecs
Mesopotamia

Publisher's Cataloging-in-Publication data
DeMocker, Michael.
   The Aztecs / Michael DeMocker.
      p. cm.
Includes bibliographic references and index.
ISBN 9781624691324
1. Aztecs—Juvenile literature. 2. Aztecs—Social life and culture—Juvenile literature. I. Series: Long ago and far away.
 F1219 2015
 972.018
                          Library of Congress Control Number: 2014945171

eBook ISBN: 9781624691331

ABOUT THE AUTHOR

Despite being a dashingly handsome, globe-trotting, award-winning photojournalist and travel writer based in New Orleans, Michael DeMocker is, in truth, really quite dull, a terrible dancer, and a frequent source of embarrassment to his wife, son, and three dogs.

PUBLISHER'S NOTE

This book has been researched in depth, and to the best of our knowledge is correct. Although every measure is taken to give an accurate account, Purple Toad Publishing makes no warranty of the accuracy of the information and is not liable for damages caused by inaccuracies.

Contents

Chapter One: From Wandering Tribe to
    Powerful Empire.................................... 4

Chapter Two: Feathers Make the Man.......10

Chapter Three: Powerful Gods,
    Ritual Sacrifices.................................12

Chapter Four: Aztec Hot Dogs
    and Worse 16

Chapter Five: Earning a Jaguar 20

Chapter Six: The Worst Job of All—Kid ... 22

Chapter Seven: You Think Football
    Is Violent 24

Chapter Eight: Unwelcome Visitors.......... 26

Further Reading 30
    Books.. 30
    On the Internet 30
    Works Consulted.................................... 30

Glossary.. 31

Index 32

From Wandering Tribe to Powerful Empire

Many centuries ago, the powerful Aztec empire dominated much of what we call Mexico today. Their society was bloodthirsty and violent, yet they also produced beautiful artwork and complex calendars, and were said to love their families very much. Plus, any civilization that brought chocolate to the world can't be all bad, right?

The origin of the Aztecs is shrouded in mystery. It is believed that a terrible drought around the year 1100 caused a tribe called the Mexica to abandon their homeland of Aztlán in the northern part of what is now Mexico. Around 1325, after about two hundred years of wandering the country looking for a permanent home, the Mexica people (who later were called the Aztecs) came to an island in the middle of Lake Texcoco.

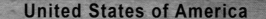

United States of America

Gulf of Mexico

Mexico

Pacific Ocean

Aztec Empire

Belize

Guatemala

Aztec Tongue Twisters

Acolhua (ah-cal-HOO-ah)

Aztlán (AHZ-lahn)

Chalchiuhtlicue (Chal-chee-weet-LEE-kway)

conquistadores (kon-KEES-tah-doors)

Huey Tlatoani (HOO-ay Tlah-tow-AH-nee)

Huitzilopochtli (wet-see-oh-POK-tlee)

Moctezuma (mawk-te-soo-mah)

pochteca (pohsh-TAY-kah)

Quetzalcoatl (kayt-sawl-KO-tal)

Tenochtitlán (Ten-oh-chit-LAN)

tonalpohualli (to-nal-po-WAL-ee)

ullamaliztli (oo-lah-ma-LEEZ-tlee)

xiuhpohualli (she-ooh-poe-AH-lee)

Legend says that their favorite god, Huitzilopochtli, appeared in a vision to their leader Tenoch, and told him to look for a pear cactus near water. On this cactus would be an eagle with a snake in its mouth, and this would be a sign for the tribe to finally stop their search for a new home. Sure enough, on a marshy, bug-infested island no one else wanted, the tribe spotted a snake-chomping eagle. It was there that the Aztecs began to build the city of Tenochtitlán. This simple settlement on a swampy island in the middle of a lake would become the center of one of history's greatest empires.

Over the first several years, the settlers built floating mud-filled islands in the lake, called chinampas. Farmers grew crops on them to feed the city. In this way, the city grew even larger as more land was created.

Canals wove between these floating islands. The Aztecs used the canals like roads. Thousands of canoes, made from hollowed-out trees, traveled the canals as the Aztecs went to work or to the market. The canoes also brought goods across the lake from neighboring cities.

The Aztecs built three bridges from their city to the mainland. The timbers they used could be removed to create impassable gaps should enemies attack the city.

From 1427 until 1430, the Aztecs fought a war with their powerful neighbors the Tepaneca, and the Aztecs won. The Tepaneca, the Aztecs, and another neighboring tribe called the Acolhua formed a triple alliance, creating an empire that would dominate the region for nearly a century.

2

Feathers Make the Man

The city of Tenochtitlán flourished. At it height, more than 200,000 people lived in the city. At its center was the sacred square where great temples for worship were built, as well as ball courts for their beloved sport, and a palace for the leader of the Aztecs, the emperor.

The emperor was the supreme ruler. The nobles, generals, and priests chose him from the royal family. He was called Huey Tlatoani, which means "the great speaker." Cities from around the empire paid tribute to the emperor in the form of jewels, cotton, feathers, and cocoa beans, which were used to make chocolate. The emperor decided when to go to war and against whom. Even the wealthy nobles dressed simply so as not to outshine the emperor. No one could look the emperor in the face, and people had to back out of the room when leaving his presence.

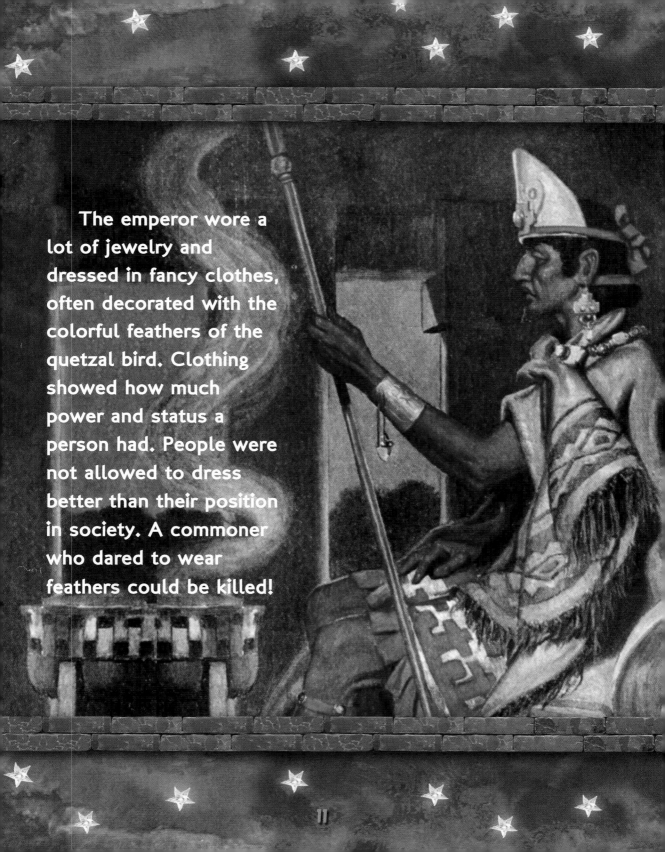

The emperor wore a lot of jewelry and dressed in fancy clothes, often decorated with the colorful feathers of the quetzal bird. Clothing showed how much power and status a person had. People were not allowed to dress better than their position in society. A commoner who dared to wear feathers could be killed!

3

Powerful Gods, Ritual Sacrifices

Speaking of killing, the Aztecs used to sacrifice people. Human sacrifices were part of the religion of the Aztecs, who believed that the sacrifices and the ceremonies appeased their powerful gods. The sacrifices took place on top of the massive Great Temple of Tenochtitlán, built in the center of the city. Some sources say that 20,000 humans were sacrificed when the temple was opened.

The Aztecs had many gods, like Tláloc, the god of rain and water; Quetzalcoatl, the god of life; and Chalchiuhtlicue, goddess of water and childbirth. Their main god was Huitzilopochtli, the god of war and the sun. Remember it was Huitzilopochtli who chose the spot on which to build Tenochtitlán, telling Tenoch to look for the snake-munching eagle.

The Aztecs believed that the sun was the most important entity in their lives, and that sacrifices must be performed to make sure the sun would rise again the next

day. They believed that the sky was a battleground between darkness and light, and if they didn't keep the sun strong with sacrifices, the world would end. The Aztecs often sacrificed warriors from other tribes to please the gods, and would fight a "flowery war" just to capture enemy soldiers to sacrifice.

Priests were vital to Aztec society. These respected men worked in pyramid-shaped temples called teocalli. They explained what the signs of nature meant, kept records in books called codices, and of course, were in charge of all the sacrifices. The priests also interpreted the round sacred stone calendar called the tonalpohualli, which kept track of which god ruled the day or the week, and what rituals must be performed. The Aztecs had a second calendar called the xiuhpohualli to keep track of the days and years.

4

Aztec Hot Dogs and Worse

Not everybody could be the emperor or a priest. While the emperor and other big shots lived in fancy houses around the sacred square, commoners lived in huts made from branches and mud. Family life was very important to the Aztecs, with many generations living under one roof. When common people died, they were often buried right under their own houses!

Unlike the rich nobles, regular people dressed more simply, with clothes made from cotton or the fibers of the maguey cactus. Men wore loincloths and cloaks, while the women wore blouses and skirts.

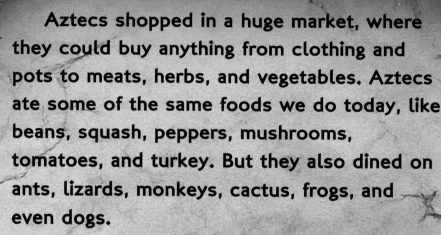

Aztecs shopped in a huge market, where they could buy anything from clothing and pots to meats, herbs, and vegetables. Aztecs ate some of the same foods we do today, like beans, squash, peppers, mushrooms, tomatoes, and turkey. But they also dined on ants, lizards, monkeys, cactus, frogs, and even dogs.

Believe it or not, the Aztecs sometimes ate other people, especially their sacrificial victims. Thankfully, their main source of food wasn't that captured guy from the next town over—it was maize, what we call corn. The Aztecs made all sorts of food from the maize grown on their farms, like tortillas, popcorn, and dumplings.

5
Earning a Jaguar

There were all kinds of jobs in the Aztec world. Warriors were admired and busy, given the number of enemy victims the priests needed. Successful warriors didn't kill their enemies—they captured them for sacrifices. The more prisoners a warrior captured, the more rewards he would get. Eventually he earned the right to wear a uniform that honored a warrior animal, like a jaguar. The best prize of all was land. The fierce Aztec warriors fought with slings, bow and arrows, and a razor-sharp wooden ax called a macuahuitl.

Talented craftsmen created jewelry, woodcarvings, pottery, and clothing. Those who worked with feathers were especially popular. Called amanteca, they made feathered headgear and clothing for the wealthy Aztecs.

Merchants, called pochteca, bought and sold goods, often traveling far and wide throughout the empire. They bought and sold jaguar skins, cocoa beans, spices, colorful feathers, and precious metals and stones.

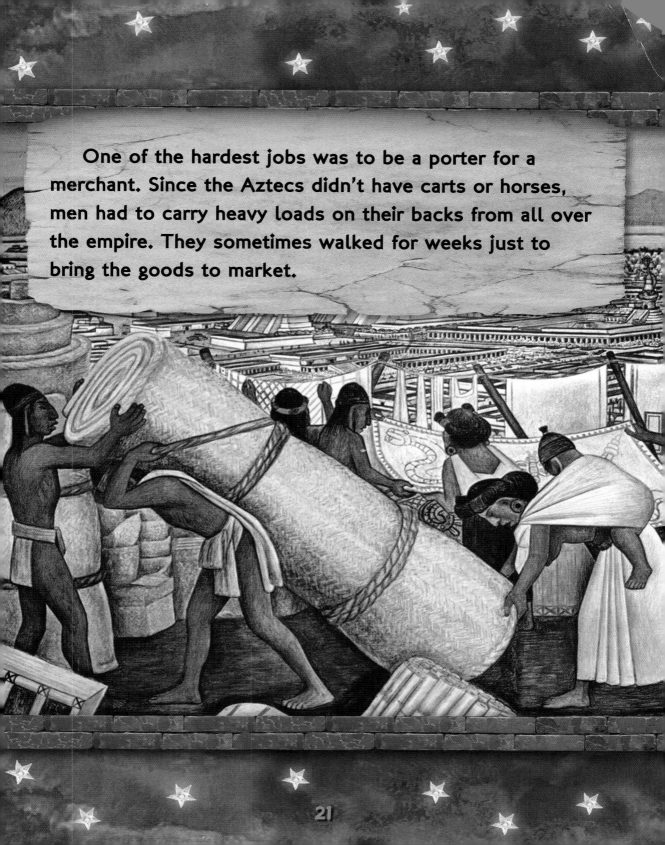

One of the hardest jobs was to be a porter for a merchant. Since the Aztecs didn't have carts or horses, men had to carry heavy loads on their backs from all over the empire. They sometimes walked for weeks just to bring the goods to market.

6

The Worst Job of All–Kid

Other Aztec jobs were fisherman, engineer, and construction worker. But one of the hardest jobs in the Aztec world was being a kid. Children in the Aztec empire worked hard. While girls stayed at home and helped with chores like weaving and cooking, the boys went to school and trained as warriors. Boys were given a shield and a bow with arrows just days after being born. WHO GIVES WEAPONS TO BABIES? The Aztecs, that's who.

It was no fun to get punished if you were an Aztec kid. And there were a lot of behaviors kids were punished for—like complaining, interrupting, and teasing. The parent would hold the offending child over burning chili peppers and make him or her breathe in the stinging smoke. That'll teach you to make faces at your teacher, pepper breath!

Even if kids didn't misbehave, they still had to put up with having their necks stretched. Parent believed that pulling on children's heads would help them grow tall. But that wasn't the worst. If a family really needed money, they could sell their healthy children to slavers.

Selling kids into slavery? Sacrificing people? Giving weapons to babies? I think it's time we change the subject to less nasty things. Like games! Yes, it wasn't all work and no play in the Aztec empire. The Aztecs loved to play (and watch) a ball game called ullamaliztli. Two teams played on a large ball court with high walls called a tlachtli. The ball court was built near the temple because the game was considered to have religious meaning. Players tried to score a point by moving a rubber ball across a line without using their hands, kind of like soccer. Stone rings were set in the wall at each end of the tlachtli, and players tried to put the ball through them, kind of like basketball. It was a very violent game and players were often injured or worse. Sometimes the leader of the losing team was even sacrificed.

WHAT? SACRIFICED? WE CAN'T EVEN TALK ABOUT GAMES WITHOUT SOMETHING NASTY HAPPENING?

Unwelcome Visitors

Even though they did some pretty nasty stuff, the Aztecs flourished. Their influence spread from the Gulf of Mexico to the Pacific Ocean, across what is now central Mexico. At their most powerful, the Aztecs were led by Emperor Moctezuma II, who ruled from 1502 until 1520. Everything was going great for them. Then, early in the 1500s, the priests saw signs of doom: a comet streaked across the sky, a temple burned down, a volcano erupted, and another temple was struck by lightning. They believed something bad was going to happen, but they didn't know what.

In 1519, a group of Spanish conquistadores, led by Hernán Cortés, arrived on horseback looking for gold and glory. The Aztecs welcomed the armor-clad conquistadores, thinking Cortés was a god. But they soon regretted being nice to the soldiers, who took their treasure and made friends with enemy tribes. The Spanish were sickened by the Aztecs' sacrifices—and they wanted Aztec gold. They declared war against the Aztecs and captured Moctezuma. The Aztec leader died soon after, although no one is sure who killed him.

In the battles that followed, the Spanish invaders were able to annihilate the Aztecs. The spears, clubs, and arrows of the Aztecs were no match for the armor, swords, and guns of the conquistadores. After defeating the Aztec warriors in battle, the Spanish destroyed the city of Tenochtitlán.

The Aztecs who were not killed by Spanish weapons later died in great numbers from the disease smallpox, which the Spanish had brought to Mexico. Other diseases, like measles, malaria, and yellow fever followed, killing even more of the Aztec people and marking the end of their powerful, and sometimes brutal, empire.

Books

Apte, Sunita. *The Aztec Empire (True Books)*. New York: Scholastic Inc., 2012.

Quick, P. S. *All About Awesome Aztecs*. Luton, United Kingdom: Andrew UK Limited, 2014.

West, David, and Anita Ganeri. *Ancient Civilizations: The Aztecs*. London: David West Children's Books, 2005.

Works Consulted

Charles River Editors. *The World's Greatest Civilizations: The History and Culture of the Aztec*. Boston: Charles River Editors, 2012.

Cóttrill, Jaime C. *Aztec History*. 2006–2013, accessed 2014. http://www.aztec-history.com.

Smith, Michael E. *The Aztecs*. Chichester, UK: Wiley-Blackwell, 2012.

On the Internet

Aztec History

    http://www.aztec-history.com/

Horrible Histories Magazine # 9: The Angry Aztecs

    http://www.horriblebooks.com/horriblehistoriesmagazines/hh09.htm

Glossary

amanteca—Aztec craftsmen who worked with feathers to make feathered headgear and clothing for wealthy Aztecs.

Chalchiuhtlicue—The Aztec goddess of childbirth.

chinampas—The floating, mud-filled islands built by the Aztecs where crops were grown.

codex—A book made mostly of pictures that records history and knowledge.

conquistador—From Spanish word for "conqueror"; adventurous soldiers from the Spanish or Portuguese empires.

flowery war—A war whose purpose was to capture the enemy for sacrifice.

Huitzilopochtli—The main god of the Aztecs, the god of war and the sun.

macuahuitl—A razor-sharp wooden ax used by Aztec warriors.

maize—Another word for corn.

Mexica—The original name of the tribe that would eventually be called the Aztecs.

pochteca—Merchants who traveled throughout the empire buying and selling their goods.

porter—Men who transported heavy loads on their backs all over the empire.

Quetzalcoatl—The Aztec god of life.

teocalli—The pyramid-shaped temples of the Aztecs.

tlachtli—The large ball court with high walls where the Aztecs played their favorite game, ullamaliztli.

Tláloc—The Aztec god of rain and water.

tonalpohualli—A round, sacred stone calendar that kept track of which Aztec god ruled the day or the week.

triple alliance—The union of the Aztec, Tepaneca, and Acolhua tribes that formed the core of the empire.

ullamaliztli—A popular ball game played on a large court where players try to score a point by moving a rubber ball across a line without using their hands, kind of like soccer.

xiuhpohualli—A round, stone 365-day calendar that kept track of days and years.

Index

Acolhua 8

amanteca 20

Aztlán 4

calendars 4, 14

canals 8

canoes 8

Chalchiuhtlicue 12

children 22

chinampas 6

chocolate 4, 10

clothing 11, 17, 20

cocoa beans 10, 20

codices 14

conquistadores 28

Cortés, Hernán 28

disease 28

emperors 10, 11, 16, 26

flowery war 14

food 19

Huitzilopochtli 6, 12

Lake Texcoco 4

macuahuitl 20

maize 19

Mexico 4, 26, 28

Moctezuma II 28

pochteca 20

porters 21

priests 14, 20, 26

quetzal bird 11

Quetzalcoatl 12

sacrifices 12, 14, 20, 25, 28

temples 10, 12, 14, 25, 26

Tenoch 6, 12

Tenochtitlán 6, 10, 12, 28

teocalli 14

Tepaneca 8

tlachtli 25

Tláloc 12

tonalpohualli 14

triple alliance 8

ullamaliztli 25

warriors 20, 22

weapons 20, 22, 28

xiuhpohualli 14

CHICKEN JOE

By Keith Grimwood, Beth Grimwood and Ezra Idlet

I got a cat
named Chicken Joe.
He sleeps with the chickens
when the weather
gets cold.

Stays warm in
the hen house all night long,
till the rooster crows at
the break of dawn.

But he's no chicken,
he's just a cat,
a cat named
Chicken Joe.

I know a little dog
named Miss Kitty.
She's a little dog
living in a great big city.

Don't want a fish,
just want a bone.
Call "Here Kitty, Kitty"
and she'll come back home.

But she's no kitty,
she's just a little dog,
a little dog named
Miss Kitty.

What's in a name? Call it what you will but it still won't change. Call it anything you want but it's still the same. What's in a name?

I heard about a parakeet
named King Kong,
tweeting and chirping
all day long.

He gets mad enough to
knock down a house in a rage.
It's a good thing he can't
get out of that cage.

He's no gorilla,
he's just a little bird,
a parakeet named
King Kong.

*What's in a name? Call it what
you will but it still won't change.
Call it anything you want but it's
still the same. What's in a name?*

Fred's got a mule
and he calls him Mister.
I'd rather kiss that mule
than kiss my sister.

Strong and steady
through rock and snow.
He'll get you where
you want to go.

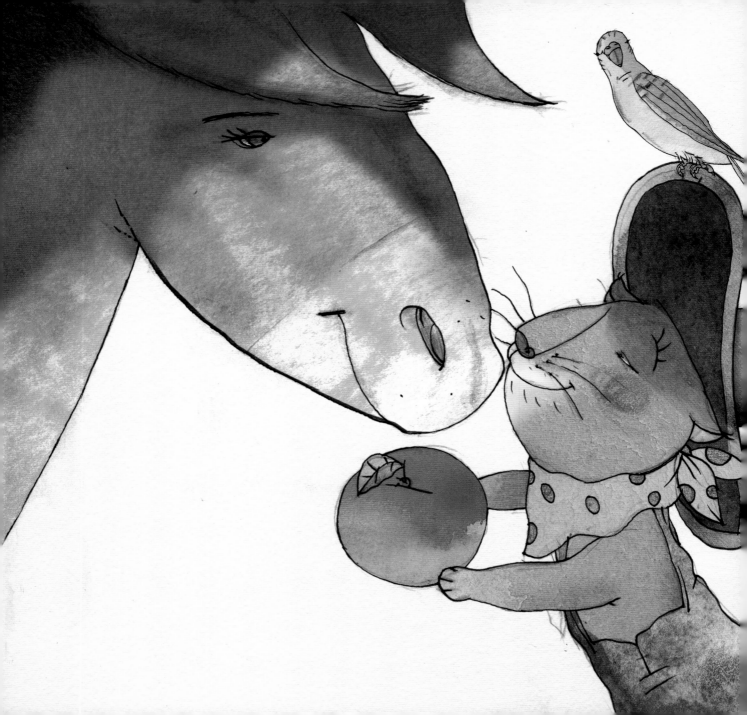

He's not a man, he's just a mule.
She's no kitty, she's just a little dog.
He's no chicken, he's just a cat,
a cat named Chicken Joe.

MY BEST DAY

By Keith Grimwood, Ezra Idlet and Fred Bogert

On my best day it's my birthday
Made a new friend at school and I'm getting all A's
I come home to a birthday surprise
My sister has been evicted and now her room is mine
My lucky day, got money in my pocket
It's snowing whipped cream and raining chocolate
On my best day we got a brand new car
A blue sparkle drum set and an electric guitar
On my best day I got two pairs of shoes
One for messing 'round and one for shooting hoops
My lucky day, got money in my pocket
It's snowing whipped cream and raining chocolate
This could never happen that's what you might say
But that's how it's gonna be on my best day

On my best day whatever needs doing is done
If it's sad it's happy, if it's boring it's fun
On my best day whatever's good is great
The clocks are all broken and there's no way to be late
My lucky day, got money in my pocket
It's snowing whipped cream and raining chocolate
This could never happen that's what you might say
But that's how it's gonna be on my best day

Hey, on my best day nobody cries
Everybody's happy and we all learn how to fly
Got my own roller coaster, got my own bumper cars
There'll be Six Flags flying over my back yard
My lucky day with all of my friends
Think about a good time that never ends
This could never happen that's what you might say
That's how it's gonna be this is my best day
This could never happen that's what you might say
That's how it's gonna be this is my best day
This could never happen that's what you might say
But that's how it's gonna be on my best day

I CAN DANCE

By Keith Grimwood and Ezra Idlet

I used to have a little problem whenever music played
I never went out to the dance floor, always stayed away
While everybody else would shake it, I was kind of shy
I sat alone all by myself and watched the fun go by
I got tired of waiting for my turn
I got up to dance
Now I can dance!

There's really nothing to it, just let your body go
Shake your arms and kick your legs
And move around the floor
It's easy, so simple, to have a real good time

When everybody sees you dancin', they want to get in line
So don't you sit there all by yourself
Just get up and dance
You can dance!

I used to have a little problem whenever music played
I never went out to the dance floor, always stayed away
While everybody else would shake it, I was kind of shy
I sat alone all by myself and watched the fun go by
Don't just sit there all by yourself

Just get up and dance
'Cause you can dance!
Look at me now
I can dance!

SOMETHING SWEET

By Keith Grimwood, James Grimwood and Ezra Idlet

Say something sweet to my baby
(Chocolate custard, pudding and pie)
Say something sweet to my boy
(Chocolate custard, pudding and pie)
His crying is driving me crazy
I don't want to hear it anymore
(Hush little baby, don't you cry)

When my baby's smiling, it lights up the town
But when my baby's crying, it turns me inside out
Say something sweet to my baby
(Chocolate custard, pudding and pie)
Say something sweet to my boy
(Chocolate custard, pudding and pie)

IT'S A PUZZLE

By Keith Grimwood, Ezra Idlet and Fred Bogert

Isn't it a puzzle that an is'll be a was?
In the middle of a muddle it'll trickle to a flood
Don't let the rain go and drizzle on your muzzle
It's a puzzle that an is'll be a was
Just a puzzle that an is'll be a was

Do you want to know why I want to go to Idaho?
I gotta go to Idaho. I haven't been there
It's excuses and saying it's no use
That keeps us from getting anywhere
Oh, isn't it a puzzle that an is'll be a was?
In the middle of a muddle it'll trickle to a flood
Don't let the rain go and drizzle on your muzzle
It's a puzzle that an is'll be a was
Just a puzzle that an is'll be a was

Is…is …till it isn't…then it was
And was …once was an is …back when it was
You can't be counting every second
But if you make sure that every second counts
Maybe might be an is in a second
Can you figure that out?

Is…is …till it isn't…then it was
And was …once was an is …back when it was
You can't be counting every second
But if you make sure that every second counts
Maybe might be an is in a second
Can you figure that out yet?

FILL IT UP

By Keith Grimwood, Beth Grimwood and Ezra Idlet

I've got an ice cream cone, I'm going to fill it up
All the way to the bottom
Chocolate, strawberry, maybe vanilla
With sprinkles if I've got 'em
1 scoop 2 scoop 3 scoop 4
If the cone was bigger then I'd have more
It's cold and sweet and such a treat
I want to live on Ice Cream Street

If you're walking into the forest
You can only walk halfway in
'Cause if you take just one more step
You'll be walking out again
1 step 2 step 3 step 4
If I lived here I'd live outdoors
It's cool and green and I can't see
The forest for the trees

Fill it up all the way to the bottom
I'm not ashamed oh and I'm not too proud
Half remembered, yeah well it's half forgotten
Halfway in is halfway out

Seems like some things used to be big
Back when I was smaller
Some things change by staying the same
Every day I get a little taller
1 inch 2 inch 3 inch 4
I'm farther and farther away from the floor
Up to the bottom and down to the top
I keep growing till I stop

Fill it up all the way to the bottom
I'm not ashamed oh and I'm not too proud
Half remembered, oh well it's half forgotten
Halfway in is halfway out

WHY I PACK MY LUNCH

By Keith Grimwood, Beth Grimwood and Ezra Idlet

The lunch bell tolls, we go bravely
To chicken knuckles with toxic gravy
Cream of tea bags, wombat pelt
Lizard lips, what's that, smelt?
Chocolate pudding that goes crunch
Is it any wonder why I pack my lunch?

French fried nostrils, tuna rolls
Is that shoe or just fillet of sole?
Grilled toenails with a side of bunions
Sautéed bats with lots of onions
Biscuits hard enough to bunt
Is it any wonder why I pack my lunch?

Some things move, some things shouldn't
You buy your lunch here? Pal, I wouldn't
Some things ought to be left alone
Turn them back to dirt and stone
Good food's rare as Haley's Comet
This stuff makes me want to… leave the table

Chunky milk, eyebrow soup
Refried snakeskin, fresh baked boot
Poultry feet with goat entrails
Escargot? No, that's snails
Chicken beaks on sticky buns
Is it any wonder why I pack my lunch?

LA LA LAND

By Keith Grimwood and Ezra Idlet

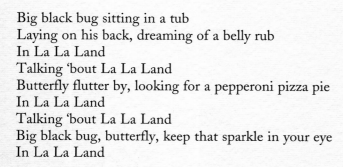

Big black bug sitting in a tub
Laying on his back, dreaming of a belly rub
In La La Land
Talking 'bout La La Land
Butterfly flutter by, looking for a pepperoni pizza pie
In La La Land
Talking 'bout La La Land
Big black bug, butterfly, keep that sparkle in your eye
In La La Land

Purple polka dotted dinosaur
Brushing his teeth with an apple core
In La La Land
Talking 'bout La La Land
Awesome possum chewing on a blossom
Hanging by his tail in an apple tree
In La La Land
Talking 'bout La La Land
Apple core, apple blossom
Whatever you want
You can bet we got some in La La Land

Saw a rhinoceros riding on a bus
With a hippo and an elephant, it's a big bus
In La La Land
Talking 'bout La La Land
Guinea pig grazing on the bathroom rug
Big black bug still dreaming of a belly rub
In La La Land
Talking 'bout La La Land
Riding on a bus, grazing on a rug
Laying on his back still dreaming of a belly rub
In La La Land

Chartreuse mongoose, cobra snake
Two straw sipping on a chocolate shake
In La La Land
Talking 'bout La La Land
Hedgehog sitting on a front porch swing
Talking on a cell phone not saying anything
In La La Land
Talking 'bout La La Land.
Close your eyes and you can see if you can think it
It can be in La La Land

BOILED OKRA AND SPINACH

By Keith Grimwood and Ezra Idlet

I woke up this morning with a smile on my face
I got dressed, made my bed, and then I picked up the place
I did what you told me, I didn't whine or cry
Took a nap, never saw time out, now all I can ask is why
Why am I being punished? Have I been so bad?
I sat down to dinner and this is what I had:
Boiled okra and spinach, it's dangerous
Fishy fish with a thousand bones, cooked in asparagus
I'd rather eat boogers than black-eyed peas
I'd trade it all for a hamburger, or a pizza with double cheese
(No anchovies, no pepperonis and no mushrooms
No black olives or any other rabbit food!)
I've got an idea that's bound to work
You finish the spinach and the black-eyed peas
Then I'll go get dessert
Ice cream, or maybe a refrigerated candy bar
I'd scream with joy for a little piece of cake
Vegetables are very good for you
Eat your fish, eat your okra too
Clean your plate, it's easy, it's just a piece of cake!

HARD BALL

By Keith Grimwood and Ezra Idlet

I wanted a hard ball, I was tired of playing softball
Wanted a hard ball, like the Major Leaguers used
I asked for a hard ball, but my parents said, "Just wait
You're only seven years old and you have to be eight"
But I wanted a hard ball in the very worst way
Needed a hard ball, I already knew how to play
I knew I would get one, they could talk and turn blue
But there was nothing they could do
Nothing they could do

I saved my pennies, saved my dimes
Collected bottles, it was summertime
The day was hot and the sky was blue
I wanted a hard ball and was gonna get one too

I had a good friend who was old enough to have one
He couldn't afford it so a partnership was made
He said he would buy it, if I had a place to hide it
I gave him my Coke-bottle fortune and got ready to play
He came back with a hard ball, we took it from the box
It was time to play hard ball, time to take our knocks
Who got to bat first? We had to be fair
I dug in my pocket and flipped a coin in the air

I lost the toss, so he was gonna hit
I started to throw. He said, "Back up a little bit"
I asked him why, he said, "I'll knock it down your throat"
I said, "You won't even see it, I bet you're gonna choke"

I let it fly, threw it as hard as I could throw
My folks were at work now, they would never know
I wanted a hard ball, it took me by surprise
When he hit the hard ball, it hit me right between the eyes
The moral of this story is to do what your parents tell you
And if you can't do that, a friend's advice might help you
If you can't do that, all is still not lost
Take a tip from me, just be lucky with the toss

COUNT ON ME

By Keith Grimwood and Ezra Idlet

Well, you can count on your fingers
And you can count on your toes
Count the freckles on your freckly face
Or the hairs in your Daddy's nose
But you can count on me, 'cause I'll always be your friend
Count on me, I'll say it time and time again

Yeah, when things get a little weird
Hey and everything goes crazy
You know I won't disappear
'Cause weird doesn't even faze me
But you can count on me through all these mixed-up days
Count on me, you know I'm never far away

There are oysters in the ocean
Making pearls from little grains of sand
And there's coal beneath the mountain that turns to diamonds
Well, I can turn your darkest night
Into the brightest day you've ever had
So count to ten if you're angry, but count on me if you're sad

Sometimes I act a little spoiled
And sometimes I lose my patience
Hey, and I can get so worked up and worried
That my good sense escapes me
But you can count on me
'Cause I can put these things behind me
Count on me, you'll always know where to find me
Count on me, 'cause I'll always be your friend

Songs performed by Trout Fishing in America (Ezra Idlet and Keith Grimwood)
Record Producer Fred Bogert except I Can Dance, Boiled Okra and Spinach and
I Can Dance – Carl Finch Artistic Director Roland Stringer Illustrator Stéphane
Jorisch Design Stéphan Lorti for Haus Design Artist Management Dick Renko
at Muzik Management/Productions Inc. (www.muzikmgt.com)

Additional artist information available at www.troutmusic.com
Master recordings under license from Trout Fishing in America
All songs published by Trout Tunes

Thank you to Karen Thom and Suzanne Renko

ISBN-10: 2-923163-49-4 / ISBN-13: 978-2-923163-49-9

Ⓒ Ⓟ 2009 Folle Avoine Productions
Ⓦ www.thesecretmountain.com

Printed in Hong Kong, China by Book Art Inc., Toronto.